T0100981

APATOSAURUS WOULD NOT MAKE A GOOD SPY

by Heather Sadler

illustrated by Steph Calvert

PICTURE WINDOW BOOKS
a capstone imprint

To my husband, Blake – the best partner I could ask for. You are my favorite adventure. –Heather

For Carole – who knows everyone like an old friend in five minutes without even being a spy. –Steph

Dinosaur Daydreams is published by
Picture Window Books, a Capstone Imprint
1710 Roe Crest Drive, North Mankato, MN 56003
www.mycapstone.com

Copyright © 2018 Picture Window Books

All rights reserved. No part of this publication may be reproduced in whole or in part, or stored in a retrieval system, or transmitted in any form or by any means, electronic, mechanical, photocopying, recording, or otherwise, without written permission of the publisher.

Library of Congress Cataloging-in-Publication data is available on the Library of Congress website.

ISBN: 978-1-5158-2128-1 (library binding)
ISBN: 978-1-5158-2132-8 (paperback)
ISBN: 978-1-5158-2140-3 (eBook PDF)

Summary: Artie Apatosaurus wants to be a secret agent, but he's much too tall to be secret! He is terrible at hiding, he can't disguise himself, and he is too slow to chase bad guys. In fact, being an Apatosaurus is exactly what makes Artie an awful spy!

Image Credit: Capstone: Jon Hughes, 23

Editor: CHRISTIANNE JONES
Designer: ASHLEE SUKER
Illustrator: STEPH CALVERT

Printed and bound in the United States of America.
2894

Greetings! Secret Agent **ARTIE** Apatosaurus here! Well, not anymore, actually. You see, being an apatosaurus is exactly what made me the worst spy ever. It's over for me, and here's why . . .

Secret agents need to use their heads – and not to smash things. They use their heads to think! I have a tiny brain, so using my head to think was a big problem.

It was hard for me to decode secret messages . . .

trick bad guys . . .

and think fast.

WHAT A DISASTER!

Agent Bossy tried to teach me how to spy on crooks.
But it's impossible to disguise yourself when you're

Instead of spying, I was the one who kept getting **SPOTTED!**

My weight was also a problem, as it really slowed me down. Being slow and bulky did not lend itself to escaping bad situations. And forget about catching the getaway car in time – I can't even fit into the agent's car !

SOUR CREAM and ONION CHIPS
CHEESE PUFFS
ROCKS COLLECTION
ICE T
MILK
PRETTY OKAY PANCAKES
SYRUP

You might say going on a diet would help me, but that's out of the question! I eat almost **880** pounds (**399** kilograms) of food a day to stay strong, so I need frequent snacks and large meals. Good spies never leave their posts, but **HOW** can I concentrate on an empty stomach?

Another problem? I don't have fingers,
and claws just don't cut it.

Pick a lock?
FORGET IT!

Hold a walkie-talkie?
NOPE!
Take notes in my spy book? I CAN'T hold the pen!
Dear Spy Diary,
This looked easier on TV.

BRONTOSAURUS BURGER
OPEN LATE
DISGUISE KIT
SPY GEAR

On top of all of that, none of the spy tools are made for dinosaurs. The binoculars, gloves, and sunglasses are all too tiny. Agent Bossy gave me an earpiece, but it didn't fit my ear! What's a spy to do without his gear? I'll give you a clue – nothing!

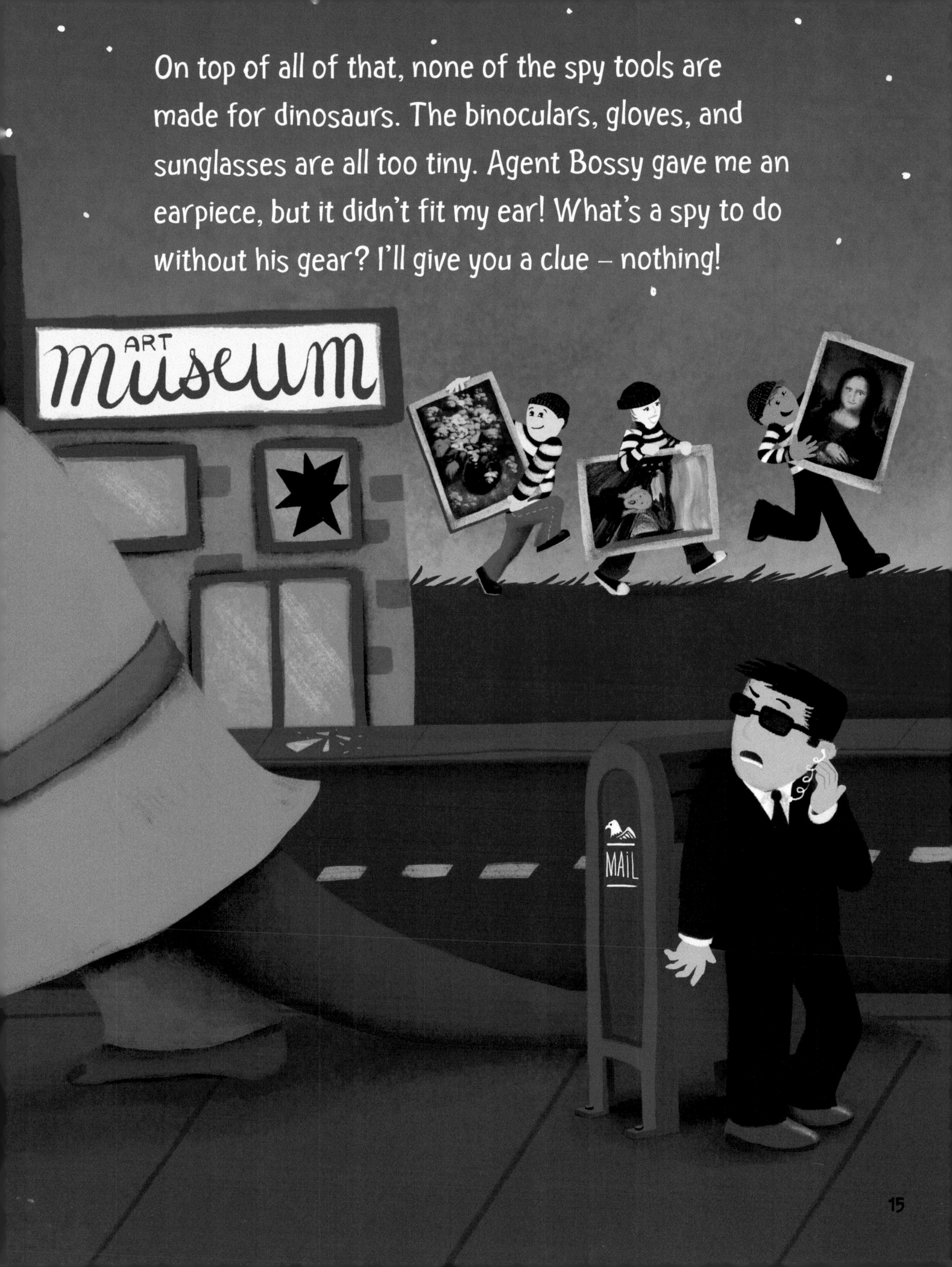

I thought I'd be great at keeping watch, but I was wrong again! My neck gets heavy, so looking left and right and up and down is very tricky. I'm just asking for a headache when I hold my head up too long!

I may be big, but I am not brave. The bad guys scare me. And when I get scared, I whip my tail, which sounds like a cannon blast. The loud noise gives away my position, and the whole city thinks there is an earthquake!

AROOOOOOOOO

Agent Bossy said I was an awful secret agent. And after looking at all the facts, I had to agree. But don't worry about me! I already have my new job picked out. Introducing **ARTIE**, the professional ice skater!

HOW TO:
STOP
STEALING
and START
SKATING
JURASSIC

DINO DIG

The answer to each question below is hidden in the art. Each answer is one word or number. Dig through the story until you find the answer. Good luck!

1. The apatosaurus lived about 146-157 million years ago. What period did they live in? (page 21)

2. Scientists wrongfully classified the apatosaurus as what other dinosaur? (page 14)

3. Apatosaurus were herbivores, eating only low-lying plants. What did they eat to help them digest plants? (page 10)

4. The size of an apatosaurus egg could be compared with what type of ball? (page 6)

5. The apatosaurus could shake the ground using what body part? (page 18)

Answer Key: 1. Jurassic 2. brontosaurus 3. rocks 4. basketball 5. tail

MORE APATOSAURUS FACTS

- *Apatosaurus* means "deceptive lizard."
- The apatosaurus was one of the largest animals to have lived on Earth.
- An apatosaurus could whip its tail so loud, it could be heard for miles! However, it was a defense mechanism and couldn't actually harm predators.
- An apatosaurus had a very thick neck that wasn't ideal for quick reactions.

DINO DISCUSSION

1. Would you rather be a secret agent or a dinosaur? Why?
2. What characteristics made Artie a bad secret agent?
3. What do you think will happen when Artie tries ice skating?

DINO GLOSSARY

bulky – big

claws – sharp curved parts on the toes or fingers of an animal

herbivore – an animal that eats only plants

SPY GLOSSARY

binoculars–a device used to see things that are far away

decode – to turn something that is written in code into ordinary language

disguise – to hide by looking like something else

earpiece – a device used to secretly listen to something

getaway –an escape